BLUE ON A BLUE PALETTE

BLUE ON A BLUE PALETTE

Poems

Lynne Thompson

AMERICAN POETS CONTINUUM SERIES. NO. 206

BOA EDITIONS, LTD. ✛ ROCHESTER, NY ✛ 2024

First Edition
23 24 25 26 7 6 5 4 3 2 1

For information about permission to reuse any material from this book, please contact The Permissions Company at www.permissionscompany.com or e-mail permdude@gmail.com.

Publications by BOA Editions, Ltd.—a not-for-profit corporation under section 501 (c) (3) of the United States Internal Revenue Code—are made possible with funds from a variety of sources, including public funds from the Literature Program of the National Endowment for the Arts; the New York State Council on the Arts, a state agency; and the County of Monroe, NY. Private funding sources include the Max and Marian Farash Charitable Foundation; the Mary S. Mulligan Charitable Trust; the Rochester Area Community Foundation; the Ames-Amzalak Memorial Trust in memory of Henry Ames, Semon Amzalak, and Dan Amzalak; the LGBT Fund of Greater Rochester; and contributions from many individuals nationwide. See Colophon on page 122 for special individual acknowledgments.

Cover Art: "Coded Message from a Symbiosome" by Darlene Charneco
Cover Design: Sandy Knight
Interior Design and Composition: Isabella Madeira
BOA Logo: Mirko

BOA Editions books are available electronically through BookShare, an online distributor offering Large-Print, Braille, Multimedia Audio Book, and Dyslexic formats, as well as through e-readers that feature text to speech capabilities.

Cataloging-in-Publication Data is available from the Library of Congress.

BOA Editions, Ltd.
250 North Goodman Street, Suite 306
Rochester, NY 14607
www.boaeditions.org
A. Poulin, Jr., Founder (1938-1996)

NYSCA

for my father, always & all ways

CONTENTS

"…some folks will tell you the blues is a woman…"
—Cornelius Eady

"…we bit our fingernails to blue buttons…"
—Dionne Brand

BLUE NIGHT WITH SCISSORS

I want to cry out my sorrow—
  this devastating fire—
as everyone lies together
with love-torn mouths and bitten souls,
lost in the round bull-ring of the moon.

(I can't look at you—or, no—
I don't want to look.)

Tell the moon to come
in the branches
of the laurel tree,
under the dusky wind,
above my shrouded heart.

Let me sleep for a moment
on fresh linens
in these tunnels of murky darkness
while scissors twirl
light in the lattices.

A CONFLUENCE OF WOMEN

—for Ida Perry

& always the sense we've assembled ourselves as
barmaids or burdens of proof,
courtesans or
drama in the style of *all's well that*
ends…as long as it doesn't end in
fine print. You might suspect us (ordinary as
gabardine) and, of course, you are right—
hell-bent as we are and
irked at our own recidivism, we
jezebels-on-the-loose, both
kenophobes and kerosene but
lastly (or mostly so), we are fearless, like to
mosey with a fret of fierce sisters who've been
nearly always misunderstood,
or worse, understood as reclining on
palanquins for others' pleasure when, in our
quiescent moments, we enjoy that leisure as our own
right to self-centered
satisfaction, the right to our own
temerity. Even a carpetbagger can't sneer at any
undertaking we women might fashion for ourselves,
vigorous as we are, quick to
whistle while drowning but not to worry: we're
xerophytic and not so easily lost as a
yacht, its tiny flags flailing, the sea the color of
zirconium, or some other form of divination.

VOICE

Say *woman*. You will slide
through a transom. Say
want or *yellow* or *terror*.
No one hears. Or say
nothing. That says it.
Say *yes* and then try
to stop saying it.

If you can't, say *no* and
poor, how poor. Say *never*,
but that's not quite it.
Say *always* and hundreds
of children will laugh
and say *Simon says* and

all of it will sound foreign
if you have forgotten how.

Say *success*, then ask
what was the question?

Say *history. Claim. Say *wild*.

A BIRTH MOTHER WEARS A COSTUME
HER DAUGHTER WILL NEVER FIT INTO

Some thought the mother said *taproot*
Some thought that woman said *resigned*

but her daughter mouthed *immaculately conceived*

Some thought the mother said *perdition*
Some thought she said *hocus pocus*

while her daughter wrote parables   wrote charms

Some hoped the daughter would say *yes, mummy*
(although they suspected the daughter said *wishbone*—

knew she would deny everything,
                              slipping into, out of)

Some never understood her need
to be alone, her fear of sorcery—they only knew her

as braid of ginger and sea salt
as weightless darling and origami

Some have heard her bark & bark & bark
Some have heard her arrange a resistance

A RAGE ON BERBICE, 1763

Before I was north and south of a new country
  I was divided from   I was a tactic   I was
  a slave-trading port
Before I was remade as Amerindian
  I was sugar as the main crop
Before I was overworked and underfed
  I was selected for immediate punishment
  "persuaded" to remain a wooden gutter for collecting rainwater
  ruled by terror and customary understandings before I was
  replenished by the arrival of two more ships
Before I was left for dead by frightened Europeans was
  before I was something black at the bottom of a buyer's cup
Before I was high upriver in the jungle
  I was silver and gold and a bounty paid to soldiers
  prepared fields farther inland   the quarters where we captives slept
I was the fort burned and abandoned before
  I joined the Arawaks and squatted with a knife in my hand
Before I was Traumatized Woman hoping to make my way
  I was the turning of the tide
Before I was awakened in the middle of the night
  I was bloodshed on the captains' bedclothes
Before I escaped the cooking pot full of Negro flesh
  before I declined to implicate the others
Before I was witness to the executions of the women rebels
  and sentenced to vigilante injustice

I was a daughter   who spelled you my name   phonetically   I was
woman with child   whose children's children   have lived   to tell you this

THE BLUE HAZE

We're like those moonstruck
 gypsy-girls who gave Apollo a one-
  eye, who coax canonical intrigue.

We are a slippery crew —
 blue in our gyre,
  blue-black like maggots

and never sexless. We invent
 a contagion when we steam,
  when we revenge.

Jesus, what an irony! —
 we women most holy
  when wet, we sister-girls

who sprinkle suspicion onto a meadow —
 phoebe babies lost to our mothers,
  quislings with no country.

We won't mark time in a vestibule.
 We can't wait to un-tame jive.
  We violet.   We violet and violet.

AMONG PEACHES

I don't care that I'm old—I still want to fuck
and I don't mean some old lady "make love"
as though I need a doily to perch my ass on.

I want to fuck with fury and sweat rolling down
the legs of us both, the mixture an emollient for
brittle bones. And if my love dog is old as I am,

I don't want him to show it or to complain or
say we have to wait for the Viagra to kick in,
for desire to erect his nipples. I want him to be

struck by a sudden urge (if I haven't been struck
first) then take me in the stockroom of Pavilion's
Market. I want to be so surprised that when I

reach out, I bring down a whole crate of peaches.
I want to bite his lip to keep him from screaming
his pleasure upon seeing my salt-and-pepper nest.

I want him to drink the *Joy* I've daubed on just
below my breasts just in case and I want him
to let me put my mouth everywhere and do what

I declined to do in my youth—& twice. I need a
nocturne to turn me around, that won't turn me
loose, to bring me to the hard edge. And when

the stock-boy comes upon us, his arms full with
boxes—the latest shipment of sweet fruit; when
he can't decide if he wants to take photos to post

on Instagram or to run away in terror, I will
tell him: *pray you get this lucky in years that will
slip off and bruise you the way peaches bruise.*

BINDINGS

Ask me—
  I will answer   *sea* (with its stony wetness
                           & far flung)

Ask *if*
  so I can answer   *myrrh* (as in our history—
                  ancient, quick kindling)

Or ask _____

  Perhaps I will   But only
                  Then again, or

Ask me to forget the answer
  as in the way of snow-melt
                 or the hidden seam

of a book's binding   Even when you don't ask

  I will demur   as in the way of Alice Coltrane

Ask again—

  I will say   *you, Torment*

SOAR (AGAIN) (BECAUSE)

it's Wednesday night, baby…
no one ever asks us.
We stand here waiting

like a field;
we make up our faces
and somewhere, a piano is playing.

The f.b.i. came to my house three weeks ago
because I've built my tower on the wings of a spider,
because I have written a good omelet.

Like my mother and her grandmother
before her, we women soar
while planes only fly patterns…

there is something,
there is nothing.
It's a journey…

THE STICKING POINT

...the sea deep as love.
                              —Mary Ruefle

Because the blue and green of it
are content.

Because I've opened my mouth
to the salt and it tastes almost

like midnight or a wound. Because
I will fall faster and lighter and

farther where there is no barrier reef
but that's not the sticking point.

See how sea enjoys a spirit of silence
in its eels, in its starfish? Because

one poet dared to write *the sea cold as*
love and knew I would ponder what

she meant: how the choices are few for
those who ignore women in revolution.

VARIATIONS ON LINES BY LINDA GREGERSON

Like the woman
  so fallen out of practice
    she can no longer

and the important
  point here
    is *practice.*

For a woman without
  practice cannot
    unbuckle, forsake the grim,

or shake the shadows.
  Or maybe the point
    is *can no longer*

as in can no longer
  be a pigeon, a snare
    with no place

in the band. To be *like*
  a woman is to be
    becoming, ever spun

around, the motto on
  an unguided path, open-
    throated. Release. & a fever.

AN UNTAMED[1] REBEL RESISTS[2] OCTAVIO ARMAND'S[3]
POEM[4] *SONETO*[5] CONSISTING[6] OF FOURTEEN[7] LINES[8]
EACH[9] ASSERTING[10] *YO*[11] *SOY*[12] *UN HOMBRE*[13] *SINCERO*[14]

1	Since the dawn of tadpoles in the bog, before//
2	the gleam radiating from your mother's eye//
3	somewhere between *hone* and *honey* and *he never knew what hit him*//
4	is everything that makes the orb revolve//
5	everything everything has evolved from—//
6	singularity—//
7	something more than individuality//
8	which is nothing less than a woman//
9	who is nothing if not true//
10	the mirror reflection of//
11	everything that is the inverse of woman//
12	she, who is *ante meridian, una mujer, woman*//
13	an antonym for a man by any other name//
14	and that's been true since the dawn of tadpoles, honey.

as just past the night sweats, there be grizzly bears, a stump
of poison oak. Then comes the clanging: women with their
frypans, metal of one driver's old Subaru versus the metal
of the egregious wealth of another. Only now and then, on air,
the cymbals, which, in Tchaikovsky's Fourth Symphony, were
stunning, but are less so when Sasha Yvchenko hears the electric
blue at Chernobyl. *Aye, and there's a rub*, Willie S. might have
said. Is the music sweet or succubus? Was the player born with
percussion dripping from just-formed fingers or is she just a
poor imitation of everyday artists, each finger wrapped with thick
gauze; fingers always pulling the trigger. *Do you hear what I hear?*
—or are you sleeping with a bee, her drone quite near your ear?
I can tell you this about bee: the colony is nothing without her, her
of the five eyes and reusable stinger, her of the serious dance moves—
hey macarena—

SELF-PORTRAIT WITHOUT CONTACT LENSES

Come morning, I feel
my way around familiar
because it isn't. I stub my toe
on a door jamb impenetrable
as Afghanistan.

How does anyone see anything—
with eyes, or with imagination?
On the street, do you notice
the vagrant who was, once,
a Golden Glove winner, or

the woman, her breasts trying
to toll time, or the sorry mother
of insufferable children?
And I fool
no one.

I am blind because I think I see you
still loving me   because dreams
are always better than whatever
should be seen: white camellias,
blue moons in a distance, indistinct.

SELF-PORTRAIT AS LAST YEAR

when I was unarticulated as mountains or months,
when there were electronic take-overs instead of
                    I loved, once.

I am delayed—as in the end of worlds,
the end being the beginning
of fissure, my body increasingly ill-defined.

Speaking of the body,
what I said of it also goes for religion,
its rituals an insistent inconstant.

                    Ditto yellow, blue,
the bitter of Brussels sprouts and
the sizzle of hot jazz, growing ever more faint.

But be sure: the sure and usual suspects (family,
other enemies, political ministers, the seeping orb)
can look me up in the funny papers.

Because you can't forget me,
write this down:

                    echo—snowmelt—suchness.

MELANCHOLIA (A DRAFT)

transformed blue flower

    *

Stop shaking.
Pretend there's a choice.

    *

The body isn't an allegory —
history doesn't fail, we fail history
while raptors' faces
hover in the storm

FRANKLY, WHEN ASKED ABOUT THE AUTONOMY OF MY BODY, I CONSIDER MY INNER ASSASSIN,

as inside me is a black-eyed animal,
the umbilicus from which everything originates—
(I have no origin story)—
unburdened by conscience, like a baby,

the umbilicus from which everything originates.
I wonder if Jesus wants souls like the Devil does:
unburdened by conscience, like a baby,
the list of pallbearers still in a drawer somewhere.

(I betcha shapeshifters want souls like devils do:
their hinges turning,
the list of pallbearers still in a drawer somewhere,
an existential jambalaya;

their hinges turning,
a clamor of voltas or
some existential jambalaya?)
My only fear: fear of a virtuous mob—

a clamor of voltas
shaped like a silver tongue.
My deepest fear?—a virtuous mob
of mother wit & mother woe.

Shaped like a silver tongue
I have no origin story
of mother wit & mother woe.
Inside me is a black-eyed animal.

SOMETIMES, THE LIGHT

(Joni Mitchell's Ode)

Blue, here is a shell for you
and sometimes, there will be sorrow,
but I have no regrets, Coyote.

We're captive on this carousel of time,
oh, but sometimes *the light.*
Blue, here is a shell for you and

varnished weeds in window jars.
Why did you pick me and
do you have any regrets, Coyote?

Buy your dreams a dollar down.
Heed the trumpets' call all night.
Blue, here is a shell for you because

the more I'm with you, pretty baby,
I'm like a black crow, flying;
dark and ragged and no regrets.

Until love sucks me back that way,
dreams…dreams and false alarms
but Blue, I've got a shell for you.
What point regrets, Coyote?

THE WAYS OF REMEMBERING WOMEN

I

Do you want to know about *the black dahlia*
or do you want the truth about Elizabeth Short?

You may not be aware: there is no such dahlia
and yet, lovers of crime focus on the dark of it,

the mystery connecting Miss Short to its rare
essence which, some say, means *enduring grace*.

I thought it was the newspapers who coined it,
eager to make a buck featuring the brutality of

that January, 1947, but no. It was the sailor men
who frequented the waterfront along the Long

Beach pier who gave the raven-haired Betty her
final moniker. They could have called her *Rose*

for the tattoo on her left calf; could have called
her *Star* for those who said she was an actress,

"well-behaved" and "sweet" despite the hideous
tableau she was found in; her torso, head, and

legs savagely detached, each from the other;
her body drained of blood; her mouth slashed

from one ear to the other. Skull pulp-like as it
roiled in the tall grass of Leimert Park. Did you

know she was pregnant, her fetus removed post-
mortem by her killer? That a Chandler—yes, one

of *those* Chandlers—was rumored to be the daddy
and still, we can't get enough of her, of anything

that made her macabre. See: *TIME* magazine,
2015, describing many confessors to her murder,

everyone looking for their mainline to notoriety.
See how, even now, you want to know *who* did it

as well as the horrific facts: Short was alive
when a butcher's knife scrolled calyx to corolla.

                    II

See how you don't remember just four years
before the Lady Dahlia, there had been another

Betty (*neé* Nuñez) although there are reasons
that you forget. She was, it is said, a *pachuca*

who hung out along Sleepy Lagoon, listened to
Central Avenue jazz and junked old folks' tales

of docile Mexicanas who sported plucked eye-
brows, darkened lips & an up-do held in place

by "rats." How many of you remember those
10 days in June, 1943? If not, re-read *News-*

week's piece not-so-subtly making judgments
about "loose girls in L.A.'s Mexican quarter";

indicting them as delinquents waylaying so-
called innocent service men with hip-swaying

& jitterbugging. "The girl-companions of zoot-
suiters" (so dubbed, whether or not it is true,

by the media, and by whites) with their own
style. Many were just girls who were forced

to testify against friends, or face detention,
or worse. Yet we only remember them, if we

recall them at all, as *mestizas*: cultural hybrids,
traitors, slaves, sell-outs; like many women

who came to L.A.—see: Nuñez and Short—
to find different identities and found them

as virgin or whore in someone's film or play,
or as the unremembered to the rest of us.

What can they ever say about what it is we
all say about them? To paraphrase an old

African: *until the lioness becomes a historian,*
some vengeful animal will always tell her story.

CALL IT HAVOC

as every step you take is clutch and coffin.
Believe me, baby-bent-on-starshine, you're
crazy if you think you can get away by train.
Doubt is your best *depend upon it*,
especially when it was only a
few days ago when you cast bread—with
glee and hope—on a mirage.
Here's a news flash: we're all chumps who
ignore the fact we live in cities of the already-dead,
justice just a fairy tale,
kingdoms bellicose,
love-sick in these times of unloving. Yes, we're all
mules. We are freak shows with mechanical limbs,
neither owners nor mortgagees.
On our rutted cheeks, the war
paint of civilizations we never
quite
remember.
So we pump the trombones, zith the zithers,
twirl amidst the ashes and tractor parts.
Under a mad magnificence, our
violence spans centuries,
wreaks havoc in suddenly-shuttered towns:
Xinjin, Zawiya, Khartoum, and
you already know what else will be lost—the River
Zuni's blue-head suckers, lifeless in this sag of bedrock.

SHASTA (AN ECHO)

Echoes are real—not imaginary.
We call out—and the land calls back.
                                        —Terry Tempest Williams

Even on a hillside covered with narcissus,
day opens its throat
to sing to the constellations: of thunder
and its lover, lighting;
of the wingswoop of a Cooper's Hawk.
Every light has its own melody:
dark in places not yet shadowed,
a full palette for the artist who thinks she is
if she could only recall the last time
she told herself that it's true.
Day's song returns again
and again whether or not we listen.
We are calmed by it. We are reminded.

Perhaps you remember the song of Castle Crags
whose granite spires look down on *Ùytaahkoo*—
the White Mountain that was renamed *Shasta*?
The mountain—formed by the fury of a volcano
two hundred million years ago—was the site
(like almost every other whose native name
has been erased) of a battle between inhabitants
and settlers who drove the locals away.

No matter.

If you climb the trailhead and go through
the mix of pine and fir and cedar, you will pass
Root Creek Trail and its eponymous watery bed.
Climb a little more, a little more. Amble among
boulders, over the flat rocks. Listen for the soft
breeze through manzanita as you gain elevation.

Call *Ùytaahkoo* until nothing's left but the timbre
of voices. Call her name. She hasn't forgotten you.

MY[1] ALCHEMISTS[2] DREAM[3] IN CURSIVE[4]

---

1   because for all of us, it's about ownership. We don't recognize value in anything that doesn't belong to us and so we fear we are impoverished. Poor we. Haven't we seen a seagull dip her wing into sun's shadow and been glad she is seagull, free and flying away from us?
2   And if we are glad, is it because we know we are rich in everything we need to be rich in; because we sense all the magic that will suffice: chemistry of light and dark, love and its seekers; the way sea is deeply deep because it hears a pygmy whale's bellow and knows that bellow is thousands of years old?
3   Perhaps you heard a narwhal, indistinctly, last night? Perhaps while you dreamed you were dreaming, she found you and made you grateful you were sleeping and thus, posed no threat to her voyage,
4   no danger to her true nature: to join—the way a poet joins one symbol to another—tail fluke to tusk; recognizing the ocean's value with neither title nor ownership, leading us to dream, as all true alchemists do…

LOS VOLCANES DE BREA

Micro-fossils: primordial woods, insects, mollusks,
seeds, and pollen grains. Covering the asphaltum:
dust, leaves, waters, old bones that darken the pit.

Rancho La Brea, once a salt mine, now Hancock Park,
is mired with the remains of tens of thousands of years.
Found during one expedition led by Sr. Portolá, 1769:

dire wolves, saber-toothed cats, pill bugs trapped in
tar geysers issuing from land-like springs. Magpies,
garter snakes, mammoths, scimitar cats. Well-kept:

trace of the La Brea woman (who probably suffered
a violent death at eighteen or twenty) ritually interred
with dog. Also found: falcons, ragweed, one Andalusian.

LOST CATHEDRALS

The future is a long time ago—preserves,
nature's trails, unending battlefields, then
your fly line rounding a bend in the river.

There's wildlife, unimpaired for generations,
and rapids and lakes versus political will
and the future being such a long time ago.

Once, Yellowstone hid itself from humans,
and the Badlands' rosy corona never ebbed;
your fly line could round every bend in the river.

In hills of bentonite clay, in petrified woods,
some petroglyphs still live yet you have to ask
why the future is such a long time ago.

Zion. Arches. Isle Royal.
Twenty-nine Palms, California.
Our future is such a long time ago. When next
will our fly lines round any bend in a river?

LAY OF A LIE

These picture-postcard palms—transplants
to Southern California—are more closely

allied with grasses than with oaks, and so
they need abundances of water to thrive

and, like the day workers who trim them,
need sustenance from elsewhere to make

them feel at home. Only the *Washingtonia*
filifera is native and it has been choked by

these imported tropical trees: the Bismark,
the Queen, the Mexican Fan. Decorative

exotics giving neither shade nor substance.
Many were planted in the 1930s to prop up

the cinematic lies we love to tell of our lives.
Meantime rats thrill palms' crowns of thatch.

RED JASPER

Swift Coronas and vintage Mercedes Benzes serenade—pistons
strumming pistons—as they cruise Highway 134. Radios blare the twin
talk-talk of the born again and arena football. James the Godfather croons
this is a man's world for the lady boomers who still believe it as they veer
south onto the 5, skirt Chavez Ravine (and every displaced Ruiz, Ramos &
Rodriguez) built into fields of faux diamonds for all the boys who pray to
play past summer. Every driver slows for the cops and eighteen-wheelers,
loops the River Los Angeles with its confessions buried in concrete under
a stubborn scent of smog, last bloom of jacarandas, and can't-squeeze-
a-drop-of-rain until tomorrow. Some of us turn north onto the 110 and
head for our weekend so there's simply no reason for all this horse-
power to come to such a hard stop just south of the Arroyo Seco except
that yesterday, minutes fell back into the groove they came from and
today, rush hour finds itself shrouded in a dark so black all we can see in
the early November sky is a Hunter's Moon, that orange-red gem, that
highwayman gathering up our lost seasons.

EVEN BEFORE THE PANDEMIC,

we were the earthquakes we fell into.
We were weather born of fire & feathers
left on the *retalbo* at San Juan Capistrano.

Look at our seas' sad kelp and eels and plastics.

Look at the alleys adorned with abandoned
        syringes, festooned with stale bread.

Where we lived,
        our children were contagious,
        their teachers were contagious,
        their playdates were full of contagion and

none of them recall when they last saw a flight
        of violet-crowned hummingbirds.

Where we lived,
        brown was & remains the color of
        our true loves' skies.

Where we lived, we laid
        in our thistle-beds over Chumash bones,
        laughing our hyena-like laughter.

And look at our miseries singing:
        There is a Fountain Filled With Blood.

BELLS

Give in to your inner goat. Do not say *I am not a goat.*
Do not say *I have only two legs.* You give milk, run with
herds, graze. Remove the latch on your mind. *Baaaaa*
in moonlight even though you will be shorn and stuffed
at a time you have not chosen. Cold days will come no
matter how many bells you wear around your neck.
Taking the long way over the meadow? Doesn't matter.
You'll reach an ivied rail where there is no way over, no
way through. This isn't anti-climax. This is the tolling.

PALE BLUES

It's not the open road we crave;
it's what hovers alongside:

red barns abandoned on a distant hill
sped by too fast;

road-kill and even more of it,
some downed

mid-lane, compelling a hard yank
of the wheel,

some lugged to the throughway's hip,
as in a gentle gesture. Silos,

forgotten, rusted. The shiny pride
of some new-age farmer and his wife

in their four-wheeler ready to lurch from
the gravel strip. Longhorns, shorthorns,

Jerseys and Belmont Reds, their tails
at rest. Angus and Holsteins gnawing

a dry culm of perennial rye grass. One
white horse, one pinto'd—no saddles,

no riders. What was once a farm could
be again with a little tending if the land

would just hint it was ready to yield. Still,
no sound but the black crows in the pale

blue of November. Suddenly comes
the chill at its seasonal verge with bare-

limbed tupelo, birch, big-tooth aspen;
a sugar maple unwilling to slope

toward death, plentiful in leaves as red
as *woo*, electrically orange, gold as new

doubloons bottom-feeding shallow creeks.
Then a dry bottom is spotted just as fast,

skirting every dip and hillock that's been
omitted from Michelin's map—grazing

the mileposts while I motor due south
to Ashland, Mount Gilead, Milllwood,

Gambier—small towns, populations just a
blip, nuts-and-rhubarb stands; Presbyterian

churches; all-grades schools, Gano grain
hoists, all shrouded beneath gray-some

clouds. Abruptly, the sun burnishes half-
warmth along the straight-line loneliness

of byways—no cars ahead, a flatbed truck
at least two miles behind. The tollroads

forsaken except for one Amish buggy,
sabled as soft-night, clip-clopping across

the overpass, coming round as my coming-
to place appears with its riot of pedestrians,

a flicker of light in the inn's welcome window.
All that was America once, fading in afterglow.

UNBRIDLED INDIANA

The desk clerk said *better go early, it's like Deliverance out there*
when I asked for a map of Putnam County's covered bridges
and was reminded of the unbridled dueling banjos
that made such a jubilation in the movie of the same name.

But when I asked for a map of Putnam County's covered bridges
all I really wanted was directions and
though I shook recalling the jubilation from the movie of the same name,
I flung my grip into a rented Accord and drove off, way too fast,

confident all I really needed was directions
to Oakalla and Dunbar Bridges.
I flung my grip into a rented Accord and drove off, way too fast,
past Greencastle's courthouse, bank of Dillinger's last coup, Walnut Creek,

looking for Oakalla and Dunbar Bridges,
looking for the kind of romance one just can't find in the city
or Greencastle's courthouse, bank of Dillinger's last coup, or Walnut Creek
(the romance one can read about in *Madame Bovary* or *Thomas & Beulah*;

the kind of romance one just won't find in the city
where, sometimes, one falls victim to madness, or to death, almost
and inexactly the kind of romance in *Madame Bovary* or *Thomas & Beulah*),
the kind of romance that isn't lurking on Highway 231 after day goes dark,

where, I've heard, one may fall victim to madness or to death.
But my mind returns to the unbridled dueling banjos
and the romance that isn't lurking on any highway after day goes dark,
that the desk clerk had said *better go early; it's like Deliverance out there*.

SNOW GEESE IN BUTTE

if you find a living snow goose, contact….
—Montana Standard, 2016

In the Treasure State, snow geese are no longer flying.
Gone quiet, their honks, their high-pitched quacks
lost over the toxic Berkeley Pit waters. The fallback
of oil jerks: *there are reasons that they're dying*
and *we're not quite ready to release the hard numbers,*
whether they exceed the three hundred found dead, 1995,
but we know that when they landed, 10,000 were alive.
One report: the lake was "white with birds" a-slumber.

We are working to keep additional birds from landing,
said an EPA adman, admitting to thousands already dead,
but not saying *the pit's full of sulfuric acid, heavy metals,*
not denying that oil crews *ignored bird hazing protocols.*
But hear the brood wail of snow geese seeking a gosling,
the hard day-and-night audible mourning for upswing?

DUCK, OUTER BANKS, NORTH CAROLINA, 2016

—for Lisa Chapkis

It may be these days, passing, but suddenly,
everything shares a history with a grist of
bones-not-quite-buried-in-sand. Fragrance of
mustangs neighing in high grass—descendants
of horses imported by a Spanish king, harnessed
by explorers who tried but failed to tame wildness
—is as miraculous as my own gamy scent. Those
explorers, fearful in a new land, ran away, but

these purebreds, their numbers waning, pose,
content to linger among the cypress stumps and
residuum of a nineteenth century hurricane,
the box and snapping turtles, purple martins,
keeping their eyes on a hungry boar nearby. We
visitors are a brown mirage who turn as pensive
as the horses, the left-behinds who see our nostrils
flare in brambles of blueberries, grapes, persimmons.

SONG FOR AFRICA LEONARD COHEN NEVER KNEW HE STARTED

Dance me very tenderly and dance me very long—

long as the river Mananara
long as the miles between the Malagasy
  and the bondsmen of Kentucky
long as memory   long as the concussions of kidnap
long as every equation plotting the distance between
  earth and its backlash   between sun and the bursting
  of hyacinth, daffodil, mustard seed,
seed most fruitless, carried across the sea, perhaps from Benin
  once misprized as French Dahomey and
  before that when the land was confused
  by the dynasty of the Edo—its people most majestic
  most black and black and black and the people are movement
  —see how they excite here   and here—
  secrets in our gardens, stunning among the periwinkle, creeping
  myrtle, confederate jasmine, floradora in spring and in summer
  when they are most *Stephanotis floribunda,* curling around
  and over and under and

have you ever seen such movement—long as the river Mananara,
  long as the miles between us and the Malagasy?

O bougarabou, dance me oh so tenderly and dance me very long

HIP OF AN ARCHIPELAGO

—for Cornelius Eady

Diamond Beach

We sailed the dhow
close to shore, the waves
slapping gently

*

One thousand dragonflies
hovered above,
raining wings on the bow

*

Above them,
planets in their orbs,
sailed, then fell still

Shela Beach

Maddie said she'd seen
a camel   somewhere
beyond the dunes

*

Beyond the dunes,
somewhere, I drank
Compari & soda

*

beside the blue
of the incomparable
Indian Ocean

*

Matondoni

The children
roasted cashews
in an oval pit

*

When they saw us,
the children cried
jambo, jambo

*

Jambo cried a sooty
gull, *jambo* yawned
the mat-maker's cat—

BLUE PLUMS, 1971

—for Judy Gottfeld

When a poet wrote, "I'd been thinking of
Greece, as I almost always am," I recalled
I had not thought of Skøpelos since being

on Skøpelos but his words made its beauty
return in a rush: nine grieving and wizened
widows keeping watch, laying in wait for us

as we sailed into the port—was it Glóssa?
Agnóntas?—every black-clad hoping to sell
us a sleeping place in their white-washeds;

the one we followed up the creaky, cobbled
stairs; the blue plums we ate upon our return
from Adrines Beach, sweet plums so content

in their skins my body rebelled then expelled
them; that first night of stars creating a light
so bright that night was no different than day.

We'd sailed there from Corfu, drunk on saliors,
ouzo; doing wheelies on vespas under an almost
moon, fresh from arriving, foolhardy, in Athens

where we'd reserved no rooms, where we were
lucky because a young Jamaican gifted us—clue-
less Americans—his flat, then left us to our own

devices only after he'd improvised a meal of orzo
& shrimp; poured retsina tasting of the Aleppo pine
resin many ancients favored, although his favor

was no favor as all we wanted was to relax by a sea
where Odysseus might have knelt. We didn't have
enough time to lay claim to the ways of the Greeks

which is the lasting lament of men and countries.
We moved on, renewed, to arrive to dark days in
Dubrovnik with its red-tiled roofs and its gothic

Rector's Palace; where young people spoke to us in
whispers because they seemed to know what was to
come; where we devoured bowls of peaches & figs

before returning to *O say can you*; photos we would
never develop, lengths of jacquard to wrap in our hair;
memories that have turned more glorious than truth.

SWALLOWS

Is that my neighbor taking her morning walk?—
yes & she tells me her husband dropped dead

while slicing Kirby cucumbers for their supper.
Is this a baroque melody she's trying to compose

of drones & earthquakes shaking the smoggy air?
When will the love I hold in my hands go to seed?

I've noticed the chicken wing I savored once
now tastes tasteless. I season it with garlic, sea salt,

bouquet garni, but the wing isn't what it once was.
In the letter box, no letters, but junk mail invites me

to attend a banquet to learn how to put my defunct
body through flames, best for everyone concerned.

I think I am afraid to weep as each of my passions
declines, dissolves, because what's left when tears go?

Once, my mother, happy in her warm socks, said
death is a part of living and *please bury me in the lilac*

silk skirt but it no longer fit when the time came. The
days darken earlier now although it is said we have

the power to change the clocks. Surely, that's not true.
Do the same swallows return each year, Capistrano?

MOSQUITOES CONSIDER TOURISTS WHO COME TO TAHITI

These tourists, lonely women mostly, come here to find
Marlon Brando (although he's been dead for years and
they should move on); to see Gauguin's *and the gold of
her bodies* (because they failed to read about his trysts

with prepubescent girls). They don't come looking for
whiners but we are ubiquitous, a drone armada of hurt
that will terrorize the women into wishing they'd left
with the sailors at the hotel bar, all of them drunk on

rum hurricanes. These women make different choices.
All they hear in the moonless night is the sound of our
excitement as we prepare to drink their blood. *Do not
shame us. Do not tell stories of our debauchery to your*

family back home. When the women leave, the Pacific
will be as blue and full of fish as when they came, our
waterfalls and jasmine will still stun. But the women's
shadows will keep fading which is why we sting them—

to savor their metallic bitterness crusting our tiny spears.

HOW CAN WE THINK OF THE MOON?

Now that we are woke,
  we are sleepier than ever.

Now that we are lit, we are
  asbestos to be got rid of.

But aren't we still *brown cow, how*?
Aren't we still pattern and 9th grade?

And what of the tides?
How will they be moved?

What of cheese?
What of the darker side

of our dreams no longer hanging
in the sky; placed solely on the face

of the *other* and maybe
on the face of another Moon.

See: Ganymede, Europa, Callisto,
the same way Hubble did—

Hubble, who had an idea
(though it never stopped the dogs

from howling   because—
and today Moon is father from).

Pink Moon. Marquee Moon. *Moon
River* (and thank you Hank Mancini).

How will sky know its neighborhoods
if its moons become gerrymandered?

What of June? Maybe May
will meet July and so let us go

to the Moon, Alice. Let us go where we
will fall again and then into moons' eyes.

AND IT SHALL BE IN THAT DAY
THAT LIVING WATERS SHALL GO OUT...

—Zechariah 14:8

The sea is over the moon.
The sea is William Grant Still
and sorry with our bones.

The sea doesn't get to vote and
mothers will always miss their daughter seas.
Sea's Galapagos Damsels are no more

so sea will call you out
and take you down
and she ain't no River Styx which is why

sea is not as blue as you and I are.
Sea, the snot-green sea, the scrotum-tightening sea
makes sea unsure who she can trust:

Sea of Japan, Sea of Azov.
Sea of Crete, Caribbean, Solomon.
See the sea divided by what men call gyres?

See the sea united by mollusks, barnacles, crabs?
Sea isn't the will of the people.
Sea cannot stop but

sea can dry up until she remembers she is
sea, separate on the surface but connected in the deep.
Seahorse. Sea lion. Sea anemone.

Sea has an attitude.
Sea is waiting for her Nobel Prize and
has a nasty habit: no survivors. Sea will swallow your ships.

ODE TO BONES

The brothers gave me the nickname *Bones*
presumably because, when they looked at me,
they thought *she is nothing but skin and* _____.

The playwright Titus Plautus gets the credit,
earned or otherwise, for saying *your name is
your destiny* but what, after all, can Romans

tell us today? Suppose instead that a name is
the past come to build a bridge to cross over?
If this is true, I could be the bones of my parents'

beloved Carib birds: a lesser Antillean tanager,
Cuban grassquit, Jamaican crow. The bones of
ancestors stolen from Africa: the Hottentot teal,

brown booby. Or, maybe after all, all bones are
just playing into the game as in the game of
dominos where the goal is to get the die from

the boneyard. On the other hand, it could be
that music makes all the difference: *this old
man, he played one…give a dog a bone….this*

*old man, he played five…with a knick-knack
paddy whack…* And never forget to look in your
kitchen—to put bones in your stock, bones to

add flavor to a mirepoix: calcium, phosphorus,
magnesium; to use a boning knife to separate
the flesh of the salmon or trout or bass. Their

bones may be small as yours or mine: strapedius
(to keep the voices in your head from driving
you crazy) or as large as the femur or tibia, each

fighting for supremacy.

SEPARATE/SEPARATE

Mother conjured me as an adjective
  before she verbed me:

    as disconnected (placenta notwithstanding)
    as discreet (thinking I would never tell)
    as distinct (in the way the outlines drawn
      around a victim of mayhem are distinct)
    as free-standing but who among my kinfolk
      was ever truly free—

Or maybe my first mother just chose:
  to disentangle
  to sever my limbs from her torso
  to sunder, let go, let God (that bitch)

See literature & law, how they enshrine dichotomy:
  A Separate Peace
  separate but equal

while some musicians propose a different riddle.
See: A Tribe Called Quest's *Separate/Together*
where *we stand great among creation*—

the process of bringing someone into existence—
the polar opposite of unmaking by separation—

the etymology made manifest as *separaten* circa 1425
just about the time the Portuguese began to traffic

in snatching the Fula and the Wolof, asleep in the teel.
Is this how the art of our disjoining became so popular

that now it's not extraordinary to remove pearls from
the oyster, to poach an elephant's tusk for her ivory?

SEEKING PARADISE

Don't tell me how I came to be born by a river. Instead, won't
you bring me honeysuckle, an applause of Mexican marigolds?
Tell me how stardust bequeaths its anthems and will not die so

you can bring me a *rebanado de cielo* that's stopped its weeping.
Tell me Sam Cooke had it right singing *a change is gonna come*
but do not tell me about a child who crossed the Rio Grande to

taste U.S. but who's been lost to her mother, doesn't know when
she will eat again. Don't you know this girl will remember and then
without warning kill you as you sleep between your twisted sheets?

∞

I wish you would bring us jalapeños baked into sweet cornbread

and with it, some green tomatoes, capers, a subtle Casa Madero.
Won't you bring us memories of a dog, a ball, or all of Saturday

to do what children want Saturday to do?

Why can't you be kind?
Why won't you imparadise us?

VOYAGE

It's another kind of *listen* I go for.
It's not new.

It's an African flame tree below wind rifle.
It's a high skies' dust-to-dust foot dance

(and I already know there's character
in its color: an elephant's bellow as cerise;

Lamu's white sea crash; aging dhows a-slap
against grey-bearded planks, also crashing).

The chordophone;
the drumbeat.

It's the surprise *whoop* of myself, sounding
like the homeland I've always never known;

like a leaf cut from its stalk; a dream of
flying, then drowning, and long affliction.

TORCH TO SHOGUN

—for Ferguson, Missouri & beyond

I saw the painting long after the world
came to know of a rebellion called Watts
in a place some call paradise; long after
I came to understand my youthful trust
had been razed to the ground, brutally, but

not so much later that I didn't recognize John
Biggers' women in *Shotgun, Third Ward #1,*
their mad backs to the artist, their shoulders
slumped with disappointment and weariness,
never-ending flames choking the blue dazzle.

DREAD IN THE SHAPE OF AI

The first time I heard the story
I seen trouble coming from a long way off
I was drinking scotch and water
I watched the Trade Center Towers
The victim lying on her side
I said "Brother, the world's on fire"

I thought I was dreaming
Saw flowers beside the railroad tracks
...so still beside my bed
The blood trail from the front door
A nightlight in the shape of a bear
...a cold fire I couldn't swallow...

AGNOSTICISM

God's angry with the world again,
unable to sleep, to pray. As the road winds,
he dines alone surrounded by reflections,

his dolls destroyed, sprawled in a pigsty.
We lay roses on his grave, listen for sounds of
cannons in rooms grotesque with furniture

of snow. Through my bedroom's window
appear puzzled faces between the dying elms,
dark as if cloven from darkness.

REVELATIONS

I quit because the rituals
became rituals, became
dark dust on the scales,
because one worshipper
kicked a mongrel the day
after she took communion…

I did love the incense—
the holies' marijuana—
and the Psalms sung by
sweet boys before the Holy

Rising of Their New Penises.
But the wafers were usually
stale, the wine was a box of
Gallo, and Solomon did threaten

both of those sniveling mothers.
I quit because my own mother
despised a frail woman
bound to a wheelchair. I quit

because I love sin—
the stink and risk of it—
no matter how many
amens absolve as well as

the velvet robes   golden
chalices   the eternal
wondering: what of Mary
Magdalene's nightly hustle;
what of a black Lazarus
denied his right to rise?

OUR ANCESTORS, ENSLAVED ONCE, SAID JUNETEENTH WOULD NEVER BE

O say can you see

but then they said

          my name is George Died-With-Your-Knee-On-My-Neck
          my name is Breonna Shot-While-Asleep-In-My-Bed
          my name is nine worshippers at Emanuel AME Church &
          my name is quite young   like Trayvon   like Tamir

they said   my name is Homer Plessy and Lloyd Gaines
          my name is Diane Nash and Myrlie Evers

they said   my name is Tulsa & Rosewood & Devil's Punchbowl, Natchez
          is Strange Fruit & Eyes Turned Toward Canada
          my name is taste of Gullah, of filé gumbo
          is scar & rice seeds, is families torn & *may I have permission*

& they
also said   my name has never been nigger-gal or -boy
          my name is Henrietta Marie, Alarm, Rattler, and
          bones & bolts waiting to be found at the bottom of the sea
            my name is Angola   my name is Senegambia

then they said

          in dawn's early light,

            we will celebrate & celebrate

                  however it is we choose to

DIRGE FOR MURDERED BLACK GIRLS

—for Breonna Taylor

How lovely the ruins.
Our beloveds. You, ever you—
(how ruined the lovely)—are

America's most unbearable fear subject to
stealth, to a Judas kiss turned ambush.
How lovely the ruins

we can't pretend we don't see: our could-have-been-
anything-they-wanted snuffed out like wicks.
How ruined the lovely.

How anguished the left behind:
the mothers, mourners, the others just like them.
How lovely the ruins,

the promise gone from *should have been*,
the girls laughing, dreaming of, calling out "see you later."
How ruined our once-lovely thoughts.

And we know this anguish continues to happen
from Chattahoochee to the City of Angels.
How ruined the lovely.
Ruins—who some think *un*lovely. How?

BOKETTO

—for Sandra Bland

I won't stop even if a cop appears from Perdition in a place he has no reason to be. Even if he slams me against the sidewalk or with the butt of his gun & tells me I am under arrest but not why, even if he looks both gleeful and hateful as he asks to see my ID then throws me into *no-one-will-ever-find-her-here*. Even if he drags me along the ground until my flesh becomes gravel road then tosses me into the backseat of a black-&-white then delivers me to a sergeant who orders a mug shot that will make me look wasted. I am not wasted. And even if, after days of being forgotten in a jail cell smelling of piss and vomit, my bladder full of fear, I am taken before someone who someone says has the right to judge me, who asks *how do you plead*, I will concede that I am only guilty of practicing *boketto*—the Japanese art of gazing into the distance with no thought of anything specific—while black.

ASSEMBLAGE

—reimagined by the artist, Betye Saar

We were born from the Time in Between
in the House of Tarot, born of Our Lady

of the Shadows and we have survived
Ten Secret Mojos:

> (We got a conjure bag; got
> good luck tokens & some herbs).

We know How to Catch a Unicorn
because we are Spirit Catchers.

We are not some High Priestess
but we have a View from the Sorcerer's Window,

have never belonged to the Black Crows in
the White Section Only. We are not one of those

Midnight Madonnas but neither are we Rainbow
Babes in the Woods. Sometimes We Dream About

Grandmother's House when it was Indigo Mercy.
Was she bequeathed us her House of the Open Hand

so we wouldn't live an Imitation of Life; so we could
live as Lullaby, Sheba, Redbone, and Black Crossing.

ONCE, WE WERE RIVERS

Would America have been America
without her Negro people?
                              —W.E.B. Du Bois

but is this the last of us?
Gone the mean barracoon.
Gone the deep wide rivers of us—

no more roosters or pickled pigs' feet.
No Aretha or *Respect*.
Is this the last of us?

Our African less African, and gone.
Our tap less Bojangles, Hines, and gone.
Gone the deep, wide rivers of us,

and gone too, our faith and fidelity
to the Betsy Ross stitch and Martin?—
was he the last of us?—

and Malcolm, Harriet, Barbara Jordan?—
all gone.   Who remains to pray
for the deep, wide rivers of us?

Gone our song and its shadow.
Gone the tongue of the Gullah.
Gone the deep, wide rivers of us—
is this the last of us?

                    *

You can't really believe that—
you've been seeing the last of us
for a long time come—

Come first the black women and their people—
Amina of Zaria, Ana de Sousa Nzinga, Nandi

Then come the transatlantic traders
sailing from Luanda, Malembo, Sierra Leone

landing Grenada, St. Vincent, St. Kitts
landing the Carolinas, Virginia, New York

Come then the black men   running   running
too many slave-named like my great-great-great
grandfather George   Fred Douglas (this is not
too old a story) see Emmitt Till   Harry Moore
four dead girls in an Alabama church   Some say

only a few bad rogues but today's cops just like
yesterday's pattyrollers shot Stephon Clark   shot
Danny Ray Thomas   shot Antwon Rose II
shot Diante Yarber   all of them   unarmed
and all this in the same year—of whose Lord?

                    *

so we fight   we fight for the last of us
even fight each other   *Ali Bomaye*

but then we hear the kora, the talking drum
the balafon and marimba
and Josephine Baker heard them
and Jacob Lawrence heard them
and Toni Morrison heard them and
Jesse Owens—running—heard the drums
that turned the Arthur Ashe racquet into a drum
the diplomacy of Ralph Bunche into a drum
the demand of Ida B. Wells into a drum
like Basquiat's *Obnoxious Liberals* was a drum
like Harriet Powers' quilting was a drum

like a Lebron James dunk is a drum
and didn't Father Curry preach
in the Church of England   like a drum
those lords and ladies had never heard before

so they know

as you know

There will never be a last of us—
(see, e.g., the Justins of Tennessee)—

We come
                We come like rivers

EARTH OMEN, EARTH OMEN,
WILL YOU BE MINE?

Scientists are full of news these days.
Trust that. Rue that.

There's neither heaven nor hell,
only earth and mystery

but none have done wrong
who still have a tongue.

In the Gospel of John, the body
and glory converge

waking so many hours before day
from the dream:

burglar music, late morning, no one home.
Yet there's a basic rhythm to everything

like a thief on tiptoe stealing into airspace
on the notes proving its provenance.

You who I cannot save,
listen to me:

the magpie is the prince of dark arts,
the albatross is always an omen.

CLASH

Not that I get the hang of our generational collage

but I resemble presdigitation when I turn thunderbolt.
I can say milk tree when I eye someone's mumbo-jumbo

while I tell you I am bone-and-drain,
make book you are common shorthand vs. exaggeration.

I am little-leaf linden.
You are someone believes.

If we were we, we would knead them—
them of the black markings.

It is everyone's last season—
a paradox inside the incredulity of cuckolds.

And the rest of us?—leapt over.

                    *

Then came you
It had to be you
I think that I
The way that we
with liberty & justice   for no one

                    *

—Jimmy Baldwin saying *people are trapped in history*
                    and history is trapped in them

—Mr. Rogers asking *won't you be my neighbor*

—Nina Simone chiding
          oh, sinner-man, where you gonna run…?

STING

I loved. Or something proximate.
He loved

but in another-ness.
Music was neither classical

nor windswept.
Breakfast was eggs, cucumber,

and we hungered
for the rest of the day.

Look for the oasis, I said.
Where's the salve for rug burn,

he asked and asked
while I counted limp petals:

he loves me, he loves,
so why has he plated the knives?

I loved, as if on a mountain
you could only find

in a thesaurus. Never fully there,
and he never felt the sting;

just left the bee to die
after its first, fatal pleasure.

LATER, I REMIND MY EX—

I am not scent of ash or
murderous in Salem County
so twig me, Crown of Thorns.

I'm not your lost letter with
feet shrunken by bathwater.
I am best when I am singing.

Call me lovely landscape as
I'm reading Baldwin and Plath
but neither Polly with a kettle

nor closing punctuation. I'm just
a wizard's witch who won't melt.
I am not *essence of is not* nor

am I extra-virgin olives & spittle.
I was never the girl some used
so forgive the somersaulting—

I'm a red, red double-decker,
a *Pink's* hot dog every blue moon.

THEY

I was a married woman,
silent as a stone in water
but not too old to dream of
the flaring of my womb,
the rigid of my jawbone.

        *

How can I explain to you:
my skin, leather black with time,
sashayed through a room of daggers.

Hard to picture those sweet boys;
hard to see them take turns,
willing to slaughter love for the company.

Mama, I could hardly breathe
and I never dreamed of love like that,
walking this earth after they

MAGDALENE BLUES

Whenever anyone says *I've found Jesus,* I always
wonder *where has Jesus been all this time* by which

I mean to ask *has Jesus been on a holiday in Machu
Picchu or in Russia's Black Dolphin Prison trying to*

convert the unconvertible? And I also mean to ask:
why is the someone who said it saying it? Is she a full-

time trollop or a woman tired of living as a legend?
This need for finding is the most curious of things.

Maybe what's been lost is something someone knew
about all along but failed to report to CNN. Or is it

something that never existed though someone always
insists it did? Like love (always an excellent bet) that's

gone lost or is only observable in the rear-view mirror
of some previously-owned Infiniti. And once found,

what's to be done with either love or Jesus? Both have
proven to be Big Mama Thornton blue yet they snag

the mind like a fear you'll burn in someone else's hell;
a worry that beloveds appear closer than they truly are.

BLUES GOT ME AND GONE

Call off the dogs; my paws are gone,
...sun has fallen behind a wooded island.

Stop the larks.
Delight me otherly

for my bones are lonely and
weeds hiss at the edge of a field.

I'm cold   cold all over,
shine upon the face of a lake...

LANGSTON WON'T STAY IN HIS GRAVE,

calls me rose of neon darkness, calls him-
self early blue evening, black smoke of
sound. Says we are related, you and I,

reminds me we are wandering in the dusk,
our faces a chocolate bar, facing the night
of two moons. And though I'm a lonely little

question mark, he laughs. Life is for the living
with gypsies and sailors. 'Til the old junk man
Death plants your feet in the cool swamp mud

shake your brown feet, honey. Wander through
this living world—get out the lunch box of your
dreams. Stay awake all night with loving or be

a woman in the doorway. Death don't ring no
doorbells or say here is that sleeping place as if
it were some noble thing. Think how thin and

sharp the moon is tonight. Don't mind dyin',
veiling what darkness hides. Haunt like mystery,
like a naked bone in gumbo. Nod at the sun.

CANTICLE AT TWILIGHT

Floating like a feather
like a single grain in the sea
grateful   despite being alive

craving grace as I crave evening
cradling rage as I cradle no vicar
I think I might just be a clock

& juju power in a terrible century
a needle & the way to plunge it in
dancing through a meadow   away

                    *

floating like singular rage
unlike twenty sheaves of feathers
like a vicar alive & dancing anyway

craving this terrible century
and every clock cradled in the sea
I think I'll always be the needle

grateful for my grain & juju power
and all the ways to plunge into it
in this meadow   just for an evening

POINSETTIAS & OTHER CONTINUUMS OF FORGETTING

Remember this irony?—*art makes order out of*
chaos. Maybe I need to write a poem about
forgetting: the annual flowering of poinsettias in
my mother's garden—the discovery that flowers
can effuse a milk children cannot drink. I remember
the day a man walked on the moon and one of us,
looking out the window, said: *I don't see anyone.*

If time is a continuum,
didn't all this happen just yesterday?

Maybe we are each a poem about forgetting—

There was a man (I don't know him anymore) who
had particular fingers, mostly squared at their tips.
He had a particular scent which remains unassigned.
He held out his hand. And what do I remember?—
he held out his hand and it was a day bright-lit as a
galvanized penny and we walked by the Pacific and
we—neither of us—remember seeing anything else.

Maybe I should write a poem about the sea.

LOST SONATA

Tonight, I am as tippery as I've ever been
as I hear the stars' contrived sonata in

a firmament with its color constantly
ebbing. I am as naked as the imbalance

of an electrical charge. Or I am swimming
along the ruined coastline of Guinea Bissau

where I am no more lost than in my own
living room. My lovers ask a trick question

and then they ask me again, babbling, daily,
differently, like every percussive instrument:

like a calabash, like a kora.
It doesn't matter. Everything is imitation—

everything is almost what it's meant to be,
my mud of a mind making papier-mâché

out of all that's unextraordinary and by now,
dear reader, you are as confused as anyone.

With that, know this: tonight I'm tippery among
fireflies—my unlovers' palms circling my want.

WHEN NOTHING ELSE WILL DO

I don't want to pluck my burr from his flesh
nor do I want to be kind Or if I am to be kind,

I want to be a kind of chameleon,
                              night-blue florescent

I want to kill that gnat on the wall
but I don't want to Hoover under
  our once-bed, site of our rub-a-dub

I don't want to be a full set
of some starlet's perfect teeth &
despite having nothing to boost, I want

to walk around wearing only my bustier
  I don't want to flower unless
  I narcissus (and yes,

  I will honor—& always—
  my fey black body, our first
  delights, and our mournings)

I want to tell his best mother everything:
  that I don't want him to ever forget
  my length of legs, both of my hands just *there*

I think I want to know what he wants
  but, perhaps, I shouldn't look in that mirror

because
  (& even *because* is a kind of want) so

just tell me—who has he been reading:
  Kafka Morrison manga for animé?

All I want is for my hair to a n e m o n e—
  & the *not wanting* to go for broke

while I drink honey bourbon and listen
  again then over again   *Not a Day Goes By*

AFTER HE LEFT I TOOK UP RESIDENCE

in a blues procession,
south of the dirty south moon.

The women wore bandannas
and shiny buckles, unfastened.

We ate meals of sautéed musk,
turtle, Prozak, and milk of ____.

In the background, muzak played
Pride & Prejudice: The Game.

Only circles, withdrawn from
drawn water, seemed strange.

The rest—the clear
morning, the switch-grass—

I drank with alacrity.
What I could not drink—

(possession
and the batting cage)—

was no cause for tears. It was
back to yesterday—to reading M.

Walker's *Lineage* at 30,000 feet—
back to things that never happen.

A WOMAN'S BODY, AGING, STILL LOVES ITSELF,

kisses the air that surrounds it, loves
the lips in full pout, famous birthplace of all kisses,
the belly, brown, round, kisses its inverted button
& the shoulders—oh, how I kiss my shoulders!—
my nose kissing lilies and a purply night sky,
my neck, long as forever, fit for twenty thousand kisses,
twenty thousand kisses for each cocoa breast and nipple,
for the lower arms that encircle each other, then kiss, kiss,
even the ears, French kissing to tunes of Django & Debussy,
the upper arms wishing to kiss their tender underarms,
thread of both hands kissing the life-line
and my cheeks colored bronze with kisses,
lashes that kiss my eyes that kiss everything they see,
my forehead a map of the places where kisses live long, long
live my kinky hair, braided with kiss after kiss after kiss…

BLUE MUSSEL

Allow yourself
to be spelled differently.
It will feel like falling.
It has waiting attached.
                    —Emma Melton

Allow yourself
everything, especially those things
you have stored on a shelf,
saying *that's not for me* or *I am not*
able. Flesh out your serpent
and your waterlily. They are similar;
they're the floor and steeple of that self
you never imagined existed.
Take a chance to stand in a shower
of your personalities. It's ok for your name

to be spelled differently
so that when you're called, you're called
agate or by those who know, *tapestry*,
or by those who are unsure *blue*
mussel because they hope you are
something more than you've seemed,
something more than just *indubitably*.
Clairvoyant, perhaps. Or something
like a body of such pure and utter
release or such unfettered gladness,

it will feel like falling.
As though the mere assignment
of a new name is a drawstring
pulling you through the grief buried
deep inside you, could be the planetary
shift that turns one woman into hardware
but turns you into a cello's bowstring.

It's as simple as child play—
so *recherché!*—
with a design so singular

it has waiting attached—
an intermission that frustrates, then propels
you to scratch to blood the itch
(that irrefutable hanker) to be
named and re-named, that desire
to be known as *seed* or *thirst* or *winter*
weather—cool but hardly detached
or unwilling—the impulse that gives you
permission to swim with a seahorse,
to admit the joy in your life is *labyrinth.*

ON RUTH STONE RELEASING THE ORB

All of life is just a way to dream of Dave Brubeck's
Blue Rondo à la Turk, of Pablo
Casals bowing Bach's *Suite No. 1* with such
duende, such
effluence that every living thing—the purple
finch eating its thistle and millet,
grown men selling cut-rate wares, children skipping rope—
halted their own joy to listen. The poet said
I am the simple sieve that drinks the universe but
just as she said so, some unsettled American
killed a Jew, an uneasy Jew killed some
Lebanese children he'd never met, their eyes turned to
Mecca, to other dominions and their schisms.
No one was listening to the music, not Chopin's
Opus No. 9, not Oscar Peterson
priming his piano with *Perdido*. Oh, how
quickly the melody fades to
riffs on revenge, to clank and helmets,
strut and baby birds with stiff wings in the desert.
Teach lessons in delight the poet might have urged, knowing
ultimately, we need to learn of sweet
verbena; the way the artist
Watanabe Kazan painted inner virtue,
Xanadu being just another color dripping from his brush.
You can live with this…
zinnias thriving in a field…*on your lips the taste of something.*

SAY *HALLELUJAH*

—for Peter J. Harris

because it strikes me: I ain't writ no praise-songs yet. I got
  laurels and a two-step platform but damn if I deserve them
    when I ain't writ no praise-songs after living long as this.

Look at this black man of happiness refusing
  to be otherwise, refusing to let any of us look
    away unless we look like we've just stepped from a pool

of joy. *He's* the joy-boy and I ain't write a single word
  of praise but time is a wizardly-woman and always on time,
    so praise the Grenadines where my folks washed up

on a strand of sand their souls returned to a long time
  come, who birthed so many generations you just have to say
    hallelujah `cause they came California and made me sequoia

and stole-from-the-Colorado-River, made me blue-eyed junco
  and Watts Towers, the Dunbar Hotel on Central Avenue and
    the Aoyama tree, ditto Central Avenue near the old Buddhist

Temple, torn down now, but praise be the Aoyama still standing,
  as well as the cactus, the jacaranda, the palm, the pine.
    Praise my misplaced pining for the paper

trees have gifted us leading me to praise the reading of books.
  Started with *Little Women* then moved on to *Cherry Ames Nurse,*
    Christie's Poirot, then anyone else required by my schooling,

and who re-reads any of them? No one. So I moved on to wanting
  to find someone who looks like me in a book. So praise Zora Neale,
    praise Pauli Murray, praise Jayne Cortez come to my college and

damn!—and praise be to becoming and didn't I become a woman
  not yet up to the challenge of my body but praise be the boys
    who thought I was.

And for this body, praise, for its transfigurations and for
  giving a middle finger to pains that try to bend it down. O & praise
    every chord of music and drum of my heart, flute ooze from my

fingertips. Praise the oboe and trumpet, and who the hell could have
  imagined a Miles or a Diz or a Shirley Horn and thank you and sweet
    journey to them all plus praise Donny Hathaway who rightly sang

giving up is hard to do putting me in mind of my brother, passed on too,
  plunking the ivories—*Mood Indigo*—which is one reason I am writing
    this praise-song for daisies, blue flax, daffodils—

meaning I praise our friendship, Mister Black-Man-of-Happiness.
  Praise, finally, for friendship's hungriest hanger-on, love. Praise for those
    I loved who didn't love me back. Praise for lovers who cannot be forgot,

for the lovers who still bring a boil to the blood, that sanguine fluid,
  crazy giver of numbered days and unnumbered regrets. Praise
    for the inhale, the ex-, little heave of chest, praise this too-short life.

NOTES

The epigraph attributed to Cornelius Eady is from his poem "I'm A Fool to Love You" (*The Autobiography of a Jukebox*). The epigraph attributed to Dionne Brand is from her poem "Ossuary I" (*Nomenclature*).

"Blue Night With Scissors" is a cento comprised of lines—or variations of them—in the works of Frederico Garcia Lorca as translated by Sarah Arvio in her collection *Poet in Spain*.

"The Blue Haze" was inspired by Terrance Hayes' poem "At Pegasus."

"Soar (again) (because)" is a cento derived from lines—or variations of them—in the poems of Sonia Sanchez in her collection *Sonia Sanchez, Collected Poems*.

"Variations on a Line by Linda Gregerson" uses lines from Gregerson's poem "Variations on a Phrase by Cormac McCarthy."

"Melancholia (a draft)" is a cento comprised of lines—or variations of them—in the poems of Carl Phillips' collection *Riding Westward*.

"Frankly, when asked about the autonomy of my body, I consider my inner assassin" is a cento composed of lines—or variations of them—in the poems of Terrance Hayes and Diane Seuss in their collections, *American Sonnets for my Past and Future Assassin* and *Frank: Sonnets*, respectively.

"sometimes, the light" is a cento comprised of Joni Mitchell lyrics.

The epigraph to "Shasta (an echo)" appears in Terry Tempest Williams' short story collection *An Unspoken Hunger*.

"My Alchemists Dream in Cursive" takes its title from the asemic writings of the poet and visual artist Sam Roxas-Chua.

The epigraph to "Song for Africa Leonard Cohen Never Knew He Started" comes from his song "Dance Me To the End of Love."

In the poem "Even Before the Pandemic," "retalbo" translates from Spanish as "altarpiece."

The italicized lines in the poem *And it shall be in that day that living waters shall go out…"* are those of James Joyce and Henry James, respectively.

In the poem "Torch to Shogun," "Shogun" is a Yoruba term meaning "God's House."

In the poem "Seeking Paradise," "rebanado de cielo" translates from Spanish as "slice of heaven."

"Dread in the Shape of Ai" is a cento comprised of lines in the poems—or variations of them—of Ai in her collection *Dread*.

"Agnosticism" is a cento comprised of first lines—or variations of them—of Robert Hayden poems.

"Dirge for Murdered Black Girls" borrows its first and third lines from Jamaal May's poem "There are Birds Here."

"Assemblage" uses the titles of several pieces of artwork by the artist Betye Saar.

"Earth Omen, Earth Omen, Will You Be Mine?" is a cento comprised of lines—or variations on them—of poetry published in *Best American Poetry 2017*.

"They" is a cento comprised of lines—or variations of them—in the poems of Kwame Dawes in his collection *Wisteria*.

"Blues got me and gone" incorporates lines from poems—or variations on them—in Theodore Roethke's *Selected Poems* and the title is taken from a line in Wanda Coleman's "Wet Thursday."

"Langston Won't Stay in His Grave," is a cento comprised of lines—or variations on them—published in Langston Hughes' *Selected Poems*.

In "On Ruth Stone Releasing the Orb," the italicized lines are from Stone's poems "The Illusion," "The Cabbage," and "At Eighty-Three She Lives Alone" published in her collection *In the Next Gallexy*.

ACKNOWLEDGMENTS

Thanks to the editors of the following publications who supported this work and publisned them—or earlier versions of them—in the following journals/publications:

Academy of American Poets: "A Birth Mother Wears a Costume Her Daughter Will Never Fit Into" [Also published in *Nelle*], "Langston Won't Stay in His Grave" [Also published in *New England Review*], "When Nothing Else Will Do" [Also published in *Massachusetts Review*];

air/light: "Boketto";

American Poetry Journal: "The Blue Haze";

Aperçus: "Unbridled Indiana";

Black Renaissance Noire: "Revelations";

Black Warrior Review: "Dread in the Shape of Ai," "My Alchemists Dream in Cursive";

Blood Orange Review: "Bells";

Cargo Literary: "Hip of an Archipelago";

COLA Catalogue, 2016: "The Ways of Remembering Women";

Catamaran: "And it shall be in that day that living waters shall go out";

Colorado Review: "Song for Africa Leonard Cohen Never Knew He Started," "Once, We Were Rivers";

Copper Nickel: "Say *hallelujah*";

Crab Orchard Review: "Shasta (an echo)";

december: "Separate/Separate";

Enchanting Verses Literary Review: "Self-Portrait as Last Year";

Foundry: "The Sticking Point";

Fourteen Hills: "Bindings";

Fox Chase Review: "Voyage";

Interliq: "Sting";

Jet Fuel Review: "Earth Omen, Earth Omen, Will You Be Mine?," "After he left I took up residence";

Kenyon Review: "Ode to Bones";

levurelitteraire.com: "Soar (again) (because)";

Literary Bohemian: "Pale Blues";

Live Encounters: "Blue Mussel";

Marsh Hawk Review: "Swallows," "Self-Portrait Without Contact Lenses";

Moria Online: "Blue Plums, 1971," "Los Volcanes de Brea";

moondance.org: "A Woman's Body, Aging,";

Nelle: "sometimes, the light";

North American Review: "Lost Sonata" [(2022) James Hearst Poetry Prize Finalist];

Pedestal: "They";

Poetrybay: "Melancholia (a draft)";

Poetry Northwest: "Agnosticism";

Red Canary Collective: "Lost Cathedrals";

Rosebud: "Assemblage," "Blue Night With Scissors," "Even Before the Pandemic";

Runes: "An untamed revel resists Octavio Armand's *Soneto* consisting of fourteen lines each asserting *yo soy un hombre sincero*";

Rust & Moth: "Seeking Paradise";

San Francisco Chronicle: "Dirge for Murdered Black Girls";

Solo Novo: "On Ruth Stone Releasing the Orb";

Sou'Wester: "Voice";

Spillway: "Call It Havoc";

Tab, A Literary Journal: "A Confluence of Women";

The Common: "A Rage on Berbice, 1763";

The Fourth River: "Snow Geese in Butte";

Torch Literary Arts: "Among Peaches";

West Trestle Review: "Duck, Outer Banks, North Carolina, 2016."

It takes a village to write, compile, and publish a collection of poems. I'm so grateful to the literary villages that support and believe in me and my poems; the poets and poetry swamis Candace Pearson and Patricia Smith; Dorothy Barresi and her Monday night poetry workshop which has been honoring poets and poetry for more than 20 years; David St. John, the bright light of a teacher who?—I'll just say who made *me* believe. I'm also grateful to current U.S. Ambassador to India and former Los Angeles Mayor Eric Garcetti who appointed me as the City's Poet Laureate as well as the Academy of American Poets who granted me a Laureate Fellowship. Also, I'm forever indebted to Aracelis Girmay who brought this manuscript to the attention of Peter Conners, Publisher of BOA Editions. Last but not least, deep appreciation to Sandy Knight, cover designer extraordinaire and to the generous Darlene Charneco, the artist who created "Coded Message from a Symbiosome." I am humbled and grateful to you all.

Finally, to family and friends too numerous to name (they know who they are and will forgive me for not naming them individually) who, despite their occasional skepticism about my commitment to poetry, have always shown up and shouted out my name to everyone in their vicinity, I love and treasure you. I wouldn't write a line without you.

ABOUT THE AUTHOR

Lynne Thompson served as the 2021-22 Poet Laureate for the City of Los Angeles and received a Laureate Fellowship from the Academy of American Poets in 2022. She received her BA from Scripps College and a JD from Southwestern School of Law. After practicing law for many years, Thompson served as the Director of Labor and Employee Relations at the University of California, Los Angeles, for twenty years. Her first collection of poems, *Beg No Pardon*, won the Perugia Press Book Prize in 2007 and the Great Lakes Colleges Association's New Writers Award in 2008. She's also the author of *Start With a Small Guitar* (What Books Press, 2013) and *Fretwork* (Marsh Hawk Books, 2019). A recipient of the George Drury Smith Award for Achievement in Poetry in 2023, she has also received fellowships from the Vermont Studio Center, Summer Literary Series (Kenya), and the City of Los Angeles. Thompson sits on the Boards of Cave Canem, The Poetry Foundation, The Los Angeles Review of Books, and Scripps College where she recently completed a four-year term as Chair of the Board of Trustees. Thompson lives in Los Angeles, California.

BOA EDITIONS, LTD. AMERICAN POETS CONTINUUM SERIES

No. 1 *The Fuhrer Bunker: A Cycle of Poems in Progress*
W. D. Snodgrass

No. 2 *She*
M. L. Rosenthal

No. 3 *Living With Distance*
Ralph J. Mills, Jr.

No. 4 *Not Just Any Death*
Michael Waters

No. 5 *That Was Then: New and Selected Poems*
Isabella Gardner

No. 6 *Things That Happen Where There Aren't Any People*
William Stafford

No. 7 *The Bridge of Change: Poems 1974–1980*
John Logan

No. 8 *Signatures*
Joseph Stroud

No. 9 *People Live Here: Selected Poems 1949–1983*
Louis Simpson

No. 10 *Yin*
Carolyn Kizer

No. 11 *Duhamel: Ideas of Order in Little Canada*
Bill Tremblay

No. 12 *Seeing It Was So*
Anthony Piccione

No. 13 *Hyam Plutzik: The Collected Poems*

No. 14 *Good Woman: Poems and a Memoir 1969–1980*
Lucille Clifton

No. 15 *Next: New Poems*
Lucille Clifton

No. 16 *Roxa: Voices of the Culver Family*
William B. Patrick

No. 17 *John Logan: The Collected Poems*

No. 18 *Isabella Gardner: The Collected Poems*

No. 19 *The Sunken Lightship*
Peter Makuck

No. 20 *The City in Which I Love You*
Li-Young Lee

No. 21 *Quilting: Poems 1987–1990*
Lucille Clifton

No. 22 *John Logan: The Collected Fiction*

No. 23 *Shenandoah and Other Verse Plays*
Delmore Schwartz

No. 24 *Nobody Lives on Arthur Godfrey Boulevard*
Gerald Costanzo

No. 25 *The Book of Names: New and Selected Poems*
Barton Sutter

No. 26 *Each in His Season*
W. D. Snodgrass

No. 27 *Wordworks: Poems Selected and New*
Richard Kostelanetz

No. 28 *What We Carry*
Dorianne Laux

No. 29 *Red Suitcase*
Naomi Shihab Nye

No. 30 *Song*
Brigit Pegeen Kelly

COLOPHON

BOA Editions, Ltd., a not-for-profit publisher of poetry
and other literary works, fosters readership and appreciation
of contemporary literature. By identifying, cultivating, and publishing
both new and established poets and selecting authors of unique literary
talent, BOA brings high-quality literature to the public.

Support for this effort comes from the sale of its publications, grant
funding, and private donations.

*The publication of this book is made possible, in part,
by the special support of the following individuals:*

Anonymous

Blue Flower Arts, LLC

Angela Bonazinga & Catherine Lewis

Bernadette Catalana

Daniel R. Cawley

Margaret B. Heminway

Nora A. Jones

Paul LaFerriere & Dorrie Parini, *in honor of Bill Waddell*

Barbara Lovenheim

Joe McElveney

Daniel M. Meyers, *in honor of J. Shepard Skiff*

John H. Schultz

Sue Stewart

William Waddell & Linda Rubel